Contents

Many, Many Mammals

There are more than 4,500 different kinds of mammals. Humans are mammals. Whales, lions, elephants, rabbits, and bats are mammals too. These animals all look different, but they have some important features in common.

Marvelous Mammals

Blue whales are mammals. They are also the largest animals that have ever lived. Like other mammals, whales breathe air. They must come to the surface of the ocean to take each breath.

Common Mammal Features

- All mammals are **vertebrates**.
- All mammals are **warm blooded**.
- All mammals have hair, fur, or wool on their body at some time.
- All female mammals feed their young on milk.
- Nearly all female mammals give birth to their young.

Bats are special mammals, because they are the only group of mammals that can fly.

Lions are meat-eating mammals. They hunt their food. Many other mammals eat plants, or both meat and plants.

3

A World of Mammals

Mammals are found all around the world. They live on land, in water, and under the ground. They can be found in thick forests, dry deserts, high mountains, and deep oceans. Each kind of mammal is suited to the place in which it lives.

Marvelous Mammals

Giraffes are mammals. They are the tallest animals in the world. Male giraffes can grow up to 18 feet tall. With their long legs and long necks, giraffes can easily reach leaves at the tops of trees.

Some mammals that live in hot places, such as the rhinoceros, have very little hair. Many mammals that live in cold places have fur to keep them warm. Polar bears have thick, white fur.

5

Mammal Senses

Mammals use their senses to find out about their world. The five senses are smell, sight, hearing, taste, and touch. However, not all mammals have all five senses. Some mammals use one sense more than the other senses. Smell is one of the most important senses for many mammals.

Marvelous Mammals

Elephants have excellent hearing. They **communicate** over long distances. They can make sounds that are too low for human ears to hear. Elephants use their trunks to touch and smell.

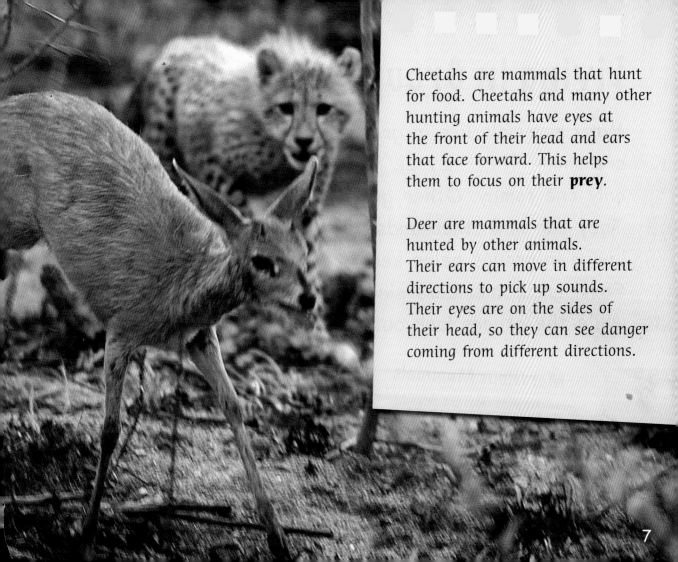

Cheetahs are mammals that hunt for food. Cheetahs and many other hunting animals have eyes at the front of their head and ears that face forward. This helps them to focus on their **prey**.

Deer are mammals that are hunted by other animals. Their ears can move in different directions to pick up sounds. Their eyes are on the sides of their head, so they can see danger coming from different directions.

Living in Groups

Many mammals live in groups. Some groups are small. They may be made up of only one family. Other groups are huge. They can have thousands of members. Living in groups helps keep mammals safe. Some group members sleep and eat while the others look out for danger.

Marvelous Mammals

Rabbits live in groups called herds. When one rabbit senses a **predator**, it thumps the ground with its hind legs. This warns the other rabbits in the herd to hop to safety.

Many mammals protect their young. Adult musk oxen form a circle around their young to protect them against predators.

Zebras and wildebeests often travel together for protection.

Mammal Mothers

All mammal mothers feed their young on milk. Mammal babies may drink their mother's milk for only a few weeks or for several years. During this time, most mammal mothers teach their babies how to find food and look out for danger.

Marvelous Mammals

Mother cheetahs teach their cubs to hunt. When the cubs reach about 18 months old, they will be able to take care of themselves.

Chimpanzee mothers take care of their babies for about six years. A mother carries her baby everywhere for the first six months.

Baby skunks live with their mothers for about six months. Even at one month old, skunks can spray a bad odor on their predators.

11

Mammals With a Difference

Mammals come in a huge variety of shapes and sizes. There are two special kinds of mammals that are very different from the rest. **Marsupials** are mammals that give birth to tiny, hairless young. **Monotremes** are mammals that lay eggs.

Marvelous Mammals

Koalas are Australian marsupials. They eat only eucalyptus leaves and hardly ever drink water. They get the liquid they need from the leaves.

Kangaroos are marsupials. Young marsupials crawl into a special pouch on their mother's belly soon after being born. They live in the pouch for several months.

There are only two kinds of monotremes: the platypus (left) and the echidna. They are both found in Australia.

13

Human Mammals

Humans are marvelous mammals. They have the ability to learn, think, and communicate. They also have invented many ways to make their lives easier and more enjoyable. Because humans are the smartest mammals, they need to protect the animals that share their world.

Marvelous Mammals

Humans are the only animals that can speak. Many other animals can use sounds to communicate. However, only humans can use language to talk about ideas.

Sometimes different kinds of mammals
work together. Specially trained dogs
can help people with disabilities
to move about and do everyday tasks.

Humans are very social
and **intelligent** mammals.

15

Glossary

communicate to tell, show, or make known

intelligent having a lot of knowledge and using it wisely

marsupial a mammal that carries its young in a pouch

monotreme a mammal that lays eggs

predator an animal that hunts and eats other animals

prey an animal that is hunted and eaten by other animals

vertebrate an animal with a backbone

warm blooded having a body temperature that stays the same no matter what the air temperature is

Index